ON THE BOATS
A Tragi-Comedy

For lovely Bernie —
who inspires me and
reminds me what matters —
and has since we first
met in 2001.
Thank you Bernie —
probably the most
generous woman
in the world.

All love
Cherry —
December,
2018

ON THE BOATS
A Tragi-Comedy

Cherry Coombe

Foreword by Anthony Seldon

The University of Buckingham Press

First published by University of Buckingham Press 2018

British Library Cataloguing in Publication Data
A catalogue record for this book is available from the British Library

ISBN 978-1-912500-07-9

Printed and bound in Great Britain by
Marston Book Services Ltd, Oxfordshire

Contents

FOREWORD

I commend these delightful poems to the reader.

Like a fine Prosecco in summer, they trickle easily through your body, leaving you gently uplifted and transported.

I declare an interest. The author is one of my team at the University of Buckingham, a brilliant teacher and inspirer of creative writing, a passionate supporter of students and staff, and our very own 'Happiness Tsar', responsible for driving forward our pioneering well-being agenda.

Many of the poems that follow reveal the author's rare combination of skill as a writer and deep human sensitivity. To me, perhaps understandably, the poem on the Boss epitomises that combination at its best.

I am delighted and honoured to recommend these poems.

Anthony Seldon

July 2018

PROLOGUE

(For Joanna Seldon)

Grace in transit
engraves a trace of love
endowing the bereft Mason
to chisel joy from rock's cold sorrow.

ACT ONE

JOINED UP WRITING

An epiphany in 73
at the top of Lardon Chase,
half way through our O levels,
peering at stars in space:
'calligraphy, geography,
plumbing, science,
philosophy, fight
opposing forces, put
fences there's no reason for,
between each field of thought;
Grammar fights analysis; French fights cookery'.
'Unless you're in the A stream,
where Latin's all you need'.
At the top of the hill
in the den that Jill
and I had dreamt our lives
we woke up to the potency
of competition's drives.
'Each school's costed on its worth.
One skill puts the other down.
Philosophers are Physics' clowns.
Evolutionists and Freud
sidled-up on libraries' shelves,
shoulder to shoulder,
facing out,
never turned to left or right
to wonder at the long held fight
between, within the disciplines,
locked up, potently.'
Today news tells us pharmacists
have no will to unlock cures
(dollars drive investors' hours);
but patients would spend
their short time left
seeking relief, for their bereft;
finding the cure for the curse
passed on, driven to succeed,
antithesis of human need.
Economies of space and time,

3

geographic draughtsmen's lines;
private water, grammar schools,
referenda carving out
small divisions, separate rules;
academic privacy, poverty and
ownership, origins and policies;
each department guarding life
from internal enemies
was locking in what might be free,
in 1973.

GOOD PROSE

(Dedicated to Long-haired Pete.)

What has happened to good prose?
Suggesting essayists are those
who read new authors and adopt
experimental turns of phrase,
and are creative, innovate?
Original's now out of date.
Who profits from the dead templates
which propagate disease, stagnate?
Abilities that are innate
are disallowed and quashed.
Why are English language freaks
free to tell you how one speaks
is inappropriate?
Instead, the language police preach
prescribed and boring plans:
kill expression; strangulate;
use a defunct, dull, repeat;
communicate in sentences
approved by an extinct elite
whose hearts had rarely missed a beat
except, perhaps, when threatened by
the challenging who asked them why
they'd spent their lives asleep.
Education's killed good prose,
ringing students through the nose
and treating them like sheep.

APOSTROPHES

I was thinking about apostrophes
and how They used to shout at me,
'Of course because it's possessive',
as if they had become obsessive
and couldn't see 'it' wasn't,
and when it was it didn't.

HOWEVER

However's a word that I've started to hate
appearing quite often in notes, of late,
sent to tell me, nice-politely
to fuck right off and not be me.

However, despite what the fearful write,
I'm not giving up on the endless fight
striving to love my own dear self,
and share my gifts with everyone else.

However, afraid, the angered love
to rain disdain from high above
it seems to me, when looking up,
they're pouring from an empty cup.

BEN OKRI

Okri's words, ours, reach,
speak, draw, take,
unteach pain, unmark life,
unjudge, make
Others ours.

DIVISIVE FIGHTS

I've had enough of lefts and rights
and, I admit, even feminists' fights,
besides all other divisive, trite,
excuses which, by their design,
blind us to what humankind
might do now and probably won't,
to keep this spinning rock afloat.
Blame's a game, which blinds us to
all that we who're here could do,
seeing that both you and I
have an impact on the sky.
I've had enough of joining in
with the chattering classes' hymn,
If you really give a fuck,
exploit your accidental luck.

RESIGNATION

Ready.
Potent.
Resting.
Waiting.
Hoping.
Opening.
Poking
Uninvited.
Spited,
Blighted,
Stunted by
Histories,
Legacies,
Reading
Lenses
Narrowing
Views,
Forming
Tunnel
Vision,
Whose?
You choose.
You lose.
Pushed
Towards
A
Tiny
Spot.
I gave my all,
My own best shot.
Goodbye,
My I.
Goodbye, you lot.

IF YOU'RE HONEST

If you're honest,
really look,
might you admit,
you drilled the hole,
screwed the hook
and hanged from it?

Look back, asking,
of your life,
cringe a bit,
who really dug your grave
and shaped your strife
to fit you for it?

Later, afterwards,
retire regret,
reflect inwardly,
see what you can salve
for prosperity:
your truth, your thirst
and those you love
(who'll thrive when they
see lives they trust
lived authentically).

A myth, 'regrets
are risks un-lived',
obscures its inverse truth.
Reflecting on regret's late risks,
organically, intuitively
inspires a wider sense of 'yet
still' Possibility.

THE ENERGY MASTER

I said, 'Excuse me, are you?'
and he beamed,
as the child of 17
living still, in me
was back in 1973,
taken in and flattered by
the man who'd held the key.

'Yes. I remember, you, Brazil,
the room, the people, energy,
the beach, after the therapy'
as I relived the jealousy:
the energy master had taken
but only just once chosen me
to sleep with him and keep
that fragile thread, in bed,
intact, knots tight,
preventing spirit's flight
from body's tapestry;
the lists of girls next chosen,
shamelessly selected
to pleasure the charlatan
had that special energy,
connections to divinity
he needed still to be
loosely in his body
and raking in the cash,
by now he's hauled a pretty stash,
from vulnerability.

The meditation master
I've since learnt to despise,
Looked straight into my eyes.
He said, 'no - please stop talking'.
Remembering is threatening
and as he walked away
he called to recent devotees,
'Don't listen to her lies'.

BOOKING.COM

I think booking dot com
was in charge of my thumb
when it clicked on the last minute deal.
'Six others just missed it,
what fuckwits, what dimwits
would pass up the chance of this steal?'
Two weeks in the sun
and nothing but fun;
reclaim from the piper you've paid
with your labour, your toil,
(your willing avail that's
made you a silly wage slave)!
Why wouldn't you choose,
when you've nothing to lose,
this chance when next it's the grave
selecting the vessel
supplying the wake
with funds you've so carefully saved?
You'll regret the mistake
if you don't book in haste,
Click now and repent, watching waves.

EVACUEES FROM '73

Evacuees from '73
Live on Corfu beside the sea
Under the skies of azure blue
Learning to be is the thing to do.
Happy as long as their 10 Euro score
Deadens the senses to all they abhor:
Commercialism, politics,
People who hit their dogs with sticks;
Women who pay to have nails painted pink;
Readers who write, others who think;
The mind, they're sure, is all that's wrong;
'don't bogart that joint, and pass on the bong'.
If you're unsettled they'll sing you a song,
Berating the worlds that the tourists come from.
Under the dazzling endless sky,
Drop the ego and learn to fly.
On Corfu where skies are blue,
Run from yourself and just be you.

FOOTBALL'S FOOTFALL

The man in his black and white striped shirt,
His shades, his shorts and watching the clock,
Striding, restless fearful of what
Happened when Iceland, pure pot luck
Strode past - looked back because I asked,
Amusing myself on holiday,
'Whose playing then today?'
'Newcastle: Watford'
'Oh right, okay,
So who do you want to win?'
He said 'are you taking the piss?'
'Just a bit'
I said, 'well Watford? Surely not, but then, I know, you know.'
'Too right. You've got it, Hen,
I've gotta get on,
The Beers to get in,
Only an hour till play'.
The man in the striped beer-logo-ed shirt
Swiftly strode away.

MANDIE

Alongside Greeks struggling to keep businesses afloat,
Refugees washed up in boats,
waiting tables fed by Tourists' welcome currency,
'Chicken and chips young man, please,
We don't eat bloody Goats';
Tropicana-Tequilla-Temptation
Displacing Ouzo, Proseco, Retsina;
Clay bathed middle-aged Thai-Chi freaks
Naked on the beach, complaining
Clothed Ex-Pats smoked straights,
she sat, face engraved by sorrow's dry knife,
clinging to the drink that oils,
makes tolerable a life,
riven through with loss,
conducting her running commentary.
'No one messes with me, No. Not me.
You know, you what I mean, yeah?
No. No one. No one messes - not me. No.'
Her hands, 'I did signing - I work. Yeah. I work, that's right.
We worked.
My sheltered, no, not sheltered. No.
Not sheltered. No. Secure.
I'll say that. Secure.
We worked. Work.
That's what we knew.
Yeah. Work, my John and me.
He was me, is me, made me Me, really.
My John made me. Yeah. He did that.
Made me. Fourteen. Sixteen.
Young really. Yeah. We met. Him and me.
Would have retired, yeah. Retired, early.
If, a week after, I'm going to tell you.
Yeah. I'll tell you my story.
It's not pretty. No. No. But I'll tell you. Yeah.'
Her new bloke, touching, supplying anaesthetic,
Beer, a vodka on the side,
The chef, here.
He, I hope, is not dying, too.
Alongside Greeks, Syrians, Tourists, Hippies,
Sits signing, drinking not dining,

Smoking straights, no one messing, no,
No one messing with her not now,
Not anyhow.
Mandie.

ON THE BOATS

You know like I were telling you, yesterday, like,
When I worked on 'boats, you know
Before I met Estelle an that,
Well, yeah, I were a bit of a lad, an that like,
An the girls you know they'd come an they'd say,
you know, like,
I wanna have a go at that Paragliding,
but I'm scared, frightened and that,
I don't wanna do it. Not sure, right.
So, you know,
I'd got all 'chat an that
I'd say,
Don't you worry, love
I'll be there,
To catch you
In 'water,
You'll be alright, with me like,
Safe, like, no worries an that,
Catch you when you're down, like,
You know,
You'll be alright with me love,
Promise you that, like,
And if you're smiling,
If you like it,
If you're happy, you know,
When you come down in 'water
Well you can buy the cocktails tonight,
And, if you don't like it, right,
If you're not smiling when I catch you, like,
well you know, I'd say,
They're on me,
I'll pay. The cocktails are on me tonight,
Like
So anyway,
I never paid for one drink that summer.
It were great, like, It were okay all that.
An I got to know,
Got my lines an that,
Knew what to say like,
Like, so anyway, there was these two, once,

Lithuania I think they come from,
And I'd got canny you know, like, by then,
Knew how to play it. You know, like.
So these two, right,
One o' them were really beautiful,
Ough, she were gorgeous,
I'm rememberin' now,
Oh God, Sorry,
Ough, she were, I dunno,
lovely like, sorry,
so, anyway, you know, like;
The other one, the ugly one,
I'd learnt how to play it by then,
you know like.
Well no, she weren't really ugly.
No. She were alright.
But I'd learnt right,
You give her some attention,
the ugly one,
Play you cards right,
An well, you know,
You'll be alright.
So, anyway, these two,
The two of them right,
Come away on their holidays, like.
You know.
They were friends like,
Nurses or I dunno, something -
let's say they worked together,
so I'd learnt right.
So, you know the cocktails an that,
That night, right,
It were going ok.
I were a lad, you know then.
Sorry? Oh, yeah, Estelle? Yeah, she knows some of it right.
No, well no, not all of it no.
I'm not daft. But I've told her enough. Right.
Anyway, right,
It were one of them nights,
So I dunno, the other one,
The lovely one,
she'd been in ' toilet or some-at,
So when she come out,

19

like, we were well, on the chair, right,
On the chair, like,
The other one
The ugly one
I'd got her right, like that an that,
Well yeah, on the chair like, you know.
It were all right, yeah. You know.
We'd started, like.
So the other one, like,
The pretty one, right,
She come out 'toilet, and she says,
Right
Well, you know, right,
She says
'What's going on here?'
Right
So I say - well, it's okay,
You're alright, love.
Don't you worry, like,
You're okay,
Join in with us if you like,
You're alright, like.
You know.
So we're right, yeah,
Well you know, right.
It were a three way that night,
And that's what it were like, right,
You know,
On the boats.
If you're smiling, like,
Same line every time. Right?
Never paid for one drink that Summer.
Yeah, it were alright that.
On the boats.

EASY LOVE

The fat man in the row to my left
had a child with no chin just like him.
The two girls in the seats to my right
stretched love's reach on the beach, every night.
A couple who knew how to live.
They didn't buy drinks,
they'd disposed of their dosh
not consuming but living to give.
It surprised me that they
had yet still to fall prey
to malaise, the sickness of most.
Those who come from the west
(and are born to excess)
can be blind to the plight of the rest.
They weren't splashing the cash
on plasticky trash
or duty free perfume and fags;
they'd memoirs and books
and flip flops and rags
in their cabin stowed holiday bags.
I have no right to moan
as I travel alone
free of relationship's fight.
I just like to hope
that my own kids don't grope
their lovers on Easy Jet flights.

ACT TWO

PASSING ON: THE BULLY'S LIFE

The bully lying, dying,
Looked straight into my eyes
He used a precious breath to warn
I'd no right of reply.

The bully gathered all his strength
To tell me we both knew
What I was like and that our child
Now knew what we knew too.

It's you, not me, that's damaged her,
I hope you've got that clear.
I've worries for our youngest child,
With you, when I'm not here.

A bully, even dying
Is not prepared to say,
'I could have been a better man
But fear got in the way'.

PASSING ON: THE BULLY'S WIFE

I was glad if he hit me.
Then it was clear.
Broken ribs, or dentistry
affirmed my own idea
that what was going on
was plain and simply
very wrong.

But then there'd be a Coventry.
He'd silently withdraw from me,
crafting my apology
through playing with my mind.

Eventually, week two or three,
he'd fold me to his chest,
stroke my hair, caress my neck,
Submission passed the test.

I was glad when he hit me.
Then it was clear.
Swollen limbs,
or bleeding skin
affirmed my new idea
that what was going on
had been my own fault
all along.

And still there'd be a Coventry.
I'd leave him morsels secretly
fuelling his recovery
while I lost my own mind.

Eventually, in 93
I packed our lives in chests
Un-plugged in time, and just before
submitting to my death.

Yet still a residue retains
a revoked memory clogs veins,

Cholesterol like, imbued, unused,
anti-fuel from poison food.

When I meet a modern bully,
(Cyber stealth, Opinionate)
Synapses link and say,
'Learned Helplessness?
Just come this way.'

THE BOSS

If elsewhere, missing;
weary, fading.
If anxious, vain;
stumbling, ill-prepared.
If kind, manipulative;
sharp, a bully.
If succeeding, poaching praise;
failing, the one to blame.
CEO, a psychopath,
if NGO a run-away,
who'd assumed the name.

SECRET PARTY

When it's coming,
and it's for you,
all they do's
ignore you;
hide behind the cabinet;
act like they've not seen you yet;
suddenly the chatter stops,
fast shot looks, convicts' hooks,
lynching those who know full well
you'd said you'd curse them all to hell,
should they rob you of the chance
to live the whole thing in advance,
keep the secret of the cast
and their story from you, last
to know the role you'll play
in their drama of your day.

TROLLS

Bully, Trolls. Pile it on
what's not then and what was wrong
lick the vacated chrysalis;
excrete what's not, and not what is;
turn back against a vibrant sky
danced by unfolding butterflies.

WOMAN EATS ALONE AND THINKS

Tap what you like on your own
Vent all your bile through your phone
Smile at my face
Deny what you hate
And fuel the mob, once alone.
Courage is quite out of vogue
Talking's for those who don't know
The internet's power
Over honesty's hour
Vent all that rage – let it go!
Today is an alien place
Where no-one can talk to a face
And notice its change
As those feelings, misplaced,
Damage, disrupt and disgrace.

VIRTUAL REALITY

Sometimes I forget
the boss is not my friend,
nor daughter confidante
and head my email 'fuck'
an accident derived
from living virtual life,
one in which I can't
erase, explain
or give another name,
rephrase, un-send,
convey the sense, instead,
that what I dread, today,
is being written off
denied a right to say,
'let me start again,
let me send my love
another way'.

QUILT

Narrative identities
internalised and felt as 'me' until
exhumed when reformed tales
of pieced and buried histories,
resurface. Reshaped selves
disintegrate internally
reordering what 'I' might be
rewoven in the tapestry
of others' unstitched lives.

The story-teller takes to bed
the fabric patterned in her head
from scraps of moments lived
and dreams a technicolor quilt,
riven through with tears and guilt
in fraying thread, stuffing unsewn,
from Comfort's childhood eiderdown.

CANCER

I said to my friend
Who's better for now
I'd buried her when she'd said
She'd cancer. And we laughed.
We laughed again about her bloke
Who goes ballistic, loses it
When traffic's at a standstill.
We pissed ourselves recounting that
She'd been quite close to fatal ill.
We laughed about our younger selves
Who thought their problems were the end
and life was really tough.
We thanked this month for bright blue skies
and blackbirds we both love.

REMEMBRANCE OF 2001

Dank November drizzle
weighted yellow gingham,
drawn to thinly framed
tear-drenched panes,
curtaining dispersing
blue light. Car doors locked.
Crackling leathering on pork;
gravy, ready, jugged, greying
grew a skin.
'Mrs Er?'
'Come in.'
'They phoned?'
'No.'
'You didn't know?'
'I do now, though.'
'But how?'
'Should we not
be pouring tea, by now?
Come in. It's cold.'
I'd had a hunch.
And someone'd called me after lunch;
his phone was in his breast pocket,
he'd phoned me last,
I'd missed the call,
they'd rung me as they'd
clasped his chest
unhooking him
to lay to rest
my second husband's sad
Remembrance,
a year since Poppy Day,
our anniversary.
Dank November drizzle,
16 bonfire nights,
darkly shadowed depths,
never laid to rest.

GRAVE RAGE

(Remembrance of 2006)

He was roaring,
'why the fuck are you alive?'
The sofa, riding back,
crashed against iron
radiating the vibration
through the central heating.
Grief, eating in the kitchen
livid with regrets,
shared the despair, aired
in the living room
with the evening news,
that ulcerated, overweight
beyond her sell by Elsie,
had voice, and time,
and life and rights,
denied to the more worthy,
dead, before their time,
dead, before they'd said,
'this is how I chime'.
Premature. Unfair.
Rage, rage, rage and rage
rage against despair.

BEFORE

Talk to me like last time.
Before.
Anxiously, as if you might hide your aside, your observation,
as if I could tell that you had made a snide critique
at the conference, of my black shoes with the blue suit.
Talk to me like last time.
Before.
Don't cross the street to avoid me
or to say hello.
Glance at me, pull your coat around your ears
and use your eyebrows to talk about the weather.
Like you did.
Before.
Carry on to the post-box just as if he might,
yet again,
neglect to send me a card.
Glance at me like last time.
Before.

GRIEF IS A HOLLOWING AIRLESS THING

Grief is a hollowing
airless thing
that breathes me,
dreads dawn,
wakes night,
resists Spring.
Grief arrests
beating hearts,
limbos us
and distances the sense of joy
from trees, danced in earth.
Grief is a random
lawless thing
that rules sense
gapes speech,
calls time,
breaks codes
and spreads a canopy of flowers
when love unearths the hour.

CHRISTMAS

A season riven through with grief,
nostalgia's gift to those who crave,
a break from putting on a face.
Brave the silence. No one speaks
of those we've buried, year on year
whose graves are empty places here
as candles lit recall the time
when we were one. The Pantomime,
'oh no she's not'

(perhaps he is)
looking down on presents, wrapped,
in last year's paper, folded, saved,
family habits passed, engraved,
economy in wanton waste
stockings stuffed to no one's taste
with presents bought in senseless haste.

Granny counting down the hours,
till she's home again, those flowers
wilting as the new year stalks
tomorrow; can't we love
in daily life, avoid the strife
invested in the vain feint hope
that Christmas will erase the pain?
Let's try a different party game,
A spade's a spade's a spade.

#RESOLUTIONS

Today on social media feeds
We're quitting the booze, the fags, the weed.
We say we hope to grow and thrive
We promise we will stay alive
Do much more than just survive.

Instead, perhaps it might be wise,
To say we'll fill that void inside
With love instead of drink
And heal the ones we leave behind
Who can't afford a shrink

ACT THREE

MOTHER'S DAY: ASHES ON LARDON CHASE

When I and my brother
threw our mother's
ashes in a shower,
over gorse and bramble
surveying childish haunts,
I wept, he shuffled an arm,
balancing an umbrella,
an awkward softening charm.
I gushed, 'she was a brilliant mum'.
He scoffed. He squeezed me tight.
'She wasn't really, was she?
But she put up a great fight.
She loved us and did all she could.
She told us that she did her best
so at least, she knew, she should.'
If it is, may her soul now rest.

REVIEWING THE VALLEY

Violet's strip of useful garden
next door to the Berkeley Smythes'
begonias, wisteria
signifying lives.

The copse where she and Jill had made
the school-girls' prototype man-cave
where red-haired-Mary couldn't find
her coveted and only friend
or means for bitter jealous kinds
of punishment for being posh;

where she and Jeremy had lost
the burden of virginity
and Roger'd sent an ambulance
to sort out the emergency
when Peter took some LSD;

her father never over it
her mother shamed, a do gooder
(the children had uncovered her
patchy, paltry parenting).

The hall and local amateurs
who didn't know they couldn't sing.

GRIEF

Honestly
I'm stricken
Riven through
With Grief
I find I weep
Suddenly
In spite of me
Embarrassingly
Breaking through
The normal things
I always do
A word or gesture
Turn of head
Glance or glass
A random phrase
Music on a radio
Something lost
From long ago
Riven through
An oak
Deep rung
Loss and Love
Are all I've sung.

CARE HOME

It came suddenly,
crept in when
the noise stopped,
remained
after the washing up;
when the bin smelt,
as the cups drained,
life waned.

What's the point of
vowing that today
and just for now,
another act of will
might save you still
for nothingness,
a waste
in space,
the empty rooms
of memory
where wishes lived
and failed?

Next door's baby wailed
and grief hollowed
the void.

FOR WALTER TULL

When he arrived, he awed me
and still does,
bringing love with him,
revealing Achilles' heel's secret,
tripping me up.
I'd thought I'd known love
and this ripped raw through
sinews,
his earth bound growth
rooted,
water born spirit
fruited fireworks,
muted by mortal-pain which
rail-roaded-roared-relentless
through us both.

And grown,
will he leave me,
home,
to grieve,
for war,
become
tomorrow's yesterday's
Lost son?

I ache,
shake,
can't sleep,
crave,
yearn,
long
for my son.

ROWAN TREE

You bolden me
You strengthen me
Reminding me
What used to be
What really was
You set me free
You tender me
Remember me
Reforming older
Newer me
Visualising
What will be
Showing me
Respectfully
Empirically
Knowingly,
In fleeting,
That after death's
Too late for love
When push comes to shove.

MAY

Outside
An undulation, raising and pitching
underpins evensong, Blackbirds, Finches,
a motorway faraway drifting in airs;
the Starlings in the roof stilled,
washing spins,
next-door's phone rings;
a dad roars,
squeals,
a trampoline;
Sheep, lamented-lambs' moans
exhausted,
settle to occasional grieving yawns;

edging clippers clank on brick-shed walls,
doors grind, in need of oil.
One-wheeled barrows thump
home.

Inside
An inculcation, raising and pitching
undermines evensong's Blackbirds, Finches,
An obsession, droning on, punctuates breath,
the worry of a roof, stilled,
thinking spins,
no one ever rings;
once we roared,
squealed,
a love machine.
Kids, lamented, goat-eared groans
out-wearied,
moved to settle, now long flown.

Skateboards cobwebbed on shed walls,
doors, closed.
One-wheeled barrows parked,
home.

ON LIVING ALONE

Hang all the laundry out to air,
Even the worst of your underwear
On the back of the dining room chairs.
Eat what you like, lick your plate.
Never say 'sorry, the dinner's late'.
Go to bed, fully clothed,
Peel off layers once the sheets aren't cold;
Never have breakfast
And never wash up,
Except for your favourite, special cup.
Stay up all night, play songs you shared,
Dance in your own private space.
Hang all your laundry out to air,
Relish Alone's embrace.

MOVING FROM A to B

Pot plants, the Christmas tree, a shed full
of garden chairs;
the paddling pool, Dad's croquet set,
an assortment of tents, those affairs:
illicit romance, a frying pan,
the Calor gas stove, no one cares;
his skateboard, a swimming-float,
tobogganing down the stairs.
Paintings, the photographs, trunks full of grandmothers' pasts,
tearfully folded in tafetta, handbags with ivory clasps;
stoat stoles and autographs,
aerogrammes posted to ask,
loved ones in austerity
list comforting everyday tasks:
'The roof leaked, the plumber's been, your Dad's got some leave, at last.'
Two cats, the Chinese clock, a rubbing from Siem Reap,
crystal glasses, wealths of books, some mother's cutlery;
maps of stop-cocks marking drama,
an umbrella, just in case.
A hairline crack in the mantelpiece
worn dark by each glance, traced.
Those Snowdrops where they shouldn't be,
always in February.
Stepping, vaulting floorboards' creak,
– moving from A to B. –

GENERATION GAP

Now, in the attic,
looking into your face
uncovered in a trunk of time
before I had a life,
I find the lines in later photographs
I carved in your sorrowing face
with youth's knife;
an unrelenting harrow
ploughing you for resources,
plundering earth,
perpetually pulling on the same patch,
depleted of mineral worth.

Now, in the attic,
looking into your face,
unmarked, untouched
your profile, mine
now in its place.
Life repents too late.

JUST THE TABLE

As it emptied
(just the table)
Time shifted left
eleven years
I didn't know,
what's written now,
on walls in pins and dents,
clues that give no evidence
of all that's happened, since.
Eleven years of change and fears
lived, faced and dissected
either side or underneath
our table, carried here
worn with loss, loves,
joys discussed;
shaped to elbows' rubbings,
toys, births, deaths, rebuffs;
steeped and yielding to the need
of those who did and those who will
pass salt, laugh, scowl,
read, eat, meet and lean on board
where life lives on in pause.
Wallpapers' archaeologists
unearth perpetual strife,
a ticking clock of must have style
rewound five times each life.
Plaster's years of
rich hewn paints
cast from deep pots,
fired at night
to change the mood,
refresh or mark a turning point,
scrape to powder,
life's in flight.
Dusty-faces,
on the table,
Time shift - right
Eleven years.

I cannot know,
what will have been,
shared and aired,
enjoyed, endured,
either side, and underneath,
Tight-grain-close-nit Oak's home board.

SUNDAY RADIO

Sunday started misty, mourning,
listening to news and scorning
what is made of yesterday's
tries to find some kinder ways
to lay the past to rest,
jeered at by the best
employed to help us to review
all the things we've tried to do
to lay our sins, attest.

Sunday went on, fog-free, lifted,
radio made way for gifted
narratives of what has been
retold as a naive dream
to heal through ill penned scores,
symphonies which opened doors
sung with all the best intentions,
harm imposed through those inventions
meant to erase flaws.

Sunday brightened, entertaining
first restoring then reframing
pictures of a rural past
never really meant to last
redrawn, coloured with a vision
in the hue of new permission
sketched to make us laugh.

Sunday, night-fall, organs roaring
fending off tomorrow's morning
ironing flat the fabric's creases
in the costumes human beasts
shape an odious camouflage.
Rise! The desert's dry mirage
offers up its peace.

RADIO ALARM

My body (whose?)
tense, awake to Morning's news,
glad, but wracked by stories told
of those whose frames
are in Baghdad,
shelled and powerless against
raging strife which won't relent;
still its sinews strain against
stress and pain and effort spent
on doing all it can to skew
what the Despots sell, while few
have purchase, or a whiff of choice,
over what grievance has rained
and buried, before chance
has gained
power over happen-stance,
still,
my bones are chilled and stiff,
tense and harbouring owned griefs
listing catalogues,
'what if'
life was lived in last night's dreams;
wishing for what hasn't been.

ON BECOMING A HAPPINESS TSAR

The kids think it's a laugh and ask,
'Is your Kimono marked
'Champion of Happiness
as well as angst and woe'?'
My sister read we'd got some dogs
to stroke when we feel low.
She texted me:
'Re Cockapoos:
Are you allowed a go?'

INDI-ZOO

Gwanny look, look Gwanny,
Gwanny look. Wolf. .
Look Gwanny Wolf,
He's eating it. Meat.
Brown bear, he's black one,
he's brown one, he's black
his tummy, itching it,
he's rubbing it, look!
Upside and downside
and nother side, look!
Baby monkey, nother one,
Mummy one, look!
That baby one tortoise is
That nother one's, come,
Carry me, up,
see it, and over it, up, up, up,
Sea lions clap. Big loud one burp.
Yellow and Gween one,
they're parrots and Red,
Red one a blue one's, McCaws
that's they're called.
Cockatoos. Tortoise poos,
Really big, look!
Day out with Indigo.
Pure story-book.

GEESE

'Did you hear that bird?'
'Quick Granny. Monsters.'
'Not in the woods, my sweet,
Listen, 'tweet tweet tweet';
Mice and worms, rabbits, Owls.'
She smiled and picked a better stick.
'That one nother one. Granny one stick.
This one Indi's. My one stick.'
Over the stile.
Across the field.
'Mummy one sheep and baby one, milks;'
'Isn't it a Daddy sheep?'
'Nother one, not. No. Baby sheeps.
Look Granny! Mummy milks. Mummy one sheeps.
Geese Granny. Look!
Tiny bird, flying gone, big one, mummy one,
Coming back. Eating it.
Geese! Granny! Look!'

ACT FOUR

ANDALUSIA

Crickets. Or electricity perhaps,
unsafe and strung across the valley;
dogs in chorus, joining the choir.
A motorbike, somewhere.
An English accent above; pool talk.
Awnings creak cracking gutters.
Hooves strain against loads,
parched roads. Church bells.
Leaves crack beneath feet.
Silence in cacophony
mirrors the unsaid
of sculled vessels
in my head.

CAROB TREE

Cover me Carob Tree
Shelter me, protect me,
Love me for being me.
Cradle me Carob Tree
Shadow me, Carry me,
Keep secrets safe for me,
Hold my new family,
Memory healing me,
Pod love from loss for me.
Set all my demons free,
Cover me Carob Tree.

Here you have let us be
Safe in our company
Broken and healingly
Lovingly humbling me.

(dedicated to Sue and Gordon Kind who know why)

BREXIT

Catch a disaffected crowd
Feed them fuel for rage
Sing them on a sunny day
Rouse them from the stage
Paint a view of me and you
Draw a hated foe
Opposite in every way
'Parasites must go!'
Gas up Crematoria.
Box up all the grey.
(All that talk of yesterday's
irrelevant today.)
Catch a disaffected crowd.
Feed them fuel for rage.
Sing them on a sunny day,
lock the bonded cage.

INDIGO'S GRANNY

Today, there were thirteen piglets,
pink and black.
'Stripey Granny, look at that!'
That's what you'd have said.
And again, when I put you to bed.
Instead, the Rellies from yesterday
wanted to visit where we used to play.
I'd never met them. They came from the blue.
I griped and complained. 'Why can't they be you?'
They say the pigs smell and they turn up their toeses.
(You'd think they'd got pig poo stuck right up their noses.)
They laughed at the ducks and the hens with the hair.
They didn't sit quietly on our little chair
and watch them until they forgot we were there.
Some other kid toured round the farm in that van
I had grabbed from the boy with a miserable gran.
I don't want to be one but sometimes it's hard
to be there alone in our old stomping yard.

YOUR ISA'S UP FOR RENEWAL

Do you want to spend
however long left
planning for the end,
filling in forms
and working out
what to invest,
once you're round the bend?
What to do with pension funds,
(Your ISA's up for renewal.)
Thinking about your NI sums,
do Ashrams' years make future's gruel?
Googling like a lunatic
to find your bus-pass
now postponed,
the rules re-jigged?

You might have spent the afternoon
dancing or just lying down
and wondering if the ceiling's lights,
might be spectral visions, might
make some sense of Being.

SINGING SIXTIES

Sing.
Too late.
Too late for pension funds,
the intent to stop,
or giving up,
for giving birth;
too late, eighth wonder of the earth;
too little left to give your back,
accounting for a lifetime's lack
of mindful application to,
all that you were born to do.
Too late for moaning and the curse
of crafting misery in verse,
compounding your compulsion that
existence owes you something back.
Too late to say, 'I'll think it over',
(Who cares if lemon's in their soda?)
Too late for vain procrastination,
Too late to conquer destination.
Too late to blow it.
Do your thing!
Too late to care,
how you should sing.

NIGHT FLIGHT

What makes me find
myself drawn,
yet still,
to all I know I cannot do
yet Will,
The idea that I might make you
and me
somehow more than what we we each can be,
quite free
of the idea
that I and you are we?
How is it that I still think of,
cleave to a dream, romantic love
when really what I dread the most
is conversation over toast
discussion of the week's routine
despite the fun shared in between?

Perhaps life's taught me: to believe
in dropping that to which we cleave;
to be a mistress of the night,
free to flee at morning's light.

AWE

Sometimes,
when the prison door
opens,
Awe,
in terror of liberty
to live out dreads
authentically,
gapes,
raw,
surprised,
aches and craves,
once more
 to be locked
inside,
imprisoned,
safe.

DARE TO LOVE

Anger, denied, harms: some freeze, cut, smoke, inject.
Fear, denied, hurts: some fight, isolate, reject.
Pain, denied, hides: some flee their sensed abject.
Love, denied, feeds instinctive drives:
to flee, to fight, to freeze and self-protect.

TINDER ME TENDERLY

Profile.
Creative type
Spends life on Skype
Twitter
Could be fitter
Cleaned the floor
When should have been
Publishing a magazine
Had deadlines not just hit her
On the day the puppy
Crapped
On the baby sitter.
Never quite
got head on right:
fritters
cash on trash
in vain attempts to trap
her youth, get back
the zest for undreamt dreams,
just before insight
flies
from unpublished reams.
Wonders why
you'd apply.
Tinder's
not just for lust,
the story goes
and otherwise,
what's up with those not on a screen,
the people who live in between
the virtual and reality,
just
here, heard, seen and touched?
Creative types
Need not apply.
But someone who can drive,
put up a shelf, who's
in good health,
domestically deaf and blind,
might find

her locked up with some words
at last the Muse unleashed
by your requests for company.
The Bard's a selfish beast

ECONOMY

(On travelling from Birmingham to Doha, on the way to Denpasar to catch a boat.)

It's easy enough for me to say,
With two of my own well on their way
To providing the world with more
But the habit of reproduction
Should be something we grow to abhor.
Flying through time, over war and despair
I know that things are no better out there
Than here in second-third class
Where my face is just inches away
as I doze
From the man with a bug up his arse;
The screen doesn't work,
His coffee's gone cold
And his laptop has gone on the blink;
This wasn't the deal
Trip Advisor had sold
And the bastards won't give him a drink.
He'd invested, you see,
his hopes and his dreams
In consumptive economy
Through which he had hoped
To pass on his schemes
To a profligate family.
To teach them to eat from a box on a seat,
Which reclines when they want to dine
To help them unwrap the inedible crap
On their way to see temples, divine.
All consume, slap and burp, fart and dress,
As their parents once did, more or less;
Our habits and customs, are used to impress
The Children who, under duress,
Conform and pass on the mess.
We are part of Biology's project
And a snake has captured the ear
With the notion that each evolution
Makes improvements, year after year.
It plays on what seems to be instinct,

74

To respond to consumptive desire,
Yet it makes little sense, if you'll let me,
To be blind to ecology's hour.

IN TRANSIT

Doha airport 28-29/12/16

In a glass box
with roaring fans
on leather sofas,
sharing greatness,
Men talk of their strategic
plans
in no-man's land.
A worn out woman
who imagines others see
a known but forgotten celebrity
they can't quite situate,
pushes alien food around a bright white plate,
in an airport lounge where you're free
to be the story you've just told
isolate from those who know
the face you don't show the world.

After quite some time of squaring up
noting he might win the game,
Paul is moved to ask a name,
and holds out his hand to Amit.
The American, a silly man
observes their singular similarity
derived from their lives of grit:
'Yes Sir. That's why we've both lost our hair.
A drink?'
'No Sir. Thank you,' Brown pinks.
A tannoy sounds; the men move on,
the woman's transit gives her time
to find this hilarious pantomime
repeated endlessly.
But surely, all those men in suits
and fabulous robes, smoking short cheroots,
must feel the same as she;
Unknown and lost in a liminal zone,
holed by anonymity

LIKE, RIGHT. LIKE, YEAH. KIND OF LIKE.

'I thought, like,
You know, like?'

'Right, sure, like,
If you don't have that
Kind of like?'

'Yeah, like, so, like
She was kind of like,
It felt like,
Like it had been like,
Like it's just not, like'

'Like, right, so
Like now,
Like, so, right?
So you guys, like?'

'Well like, I like
You know, we talked like,
But's it's like?'

'Yeah right, like.'

'I feel, like, you know right?'

'Like, yeah so like
It's not really amazing, like,
So?'

'Yeah, like'

'So you're kind of stuck like,
Like that now, right, like,
Like in limbo, like?'

'Yeah, right, yeah, like Like yeah.
Like you know yeah

The energy, like?'

'So you don't have,
Like, that, like,
Kind of energy right, like?'

'So yeah – like right – yeah
Like, I'll be kind of like,
How can we be like?'

'Like kind of keep like that,
With like, like all that crap? Like, so?'

'Yeah, sure, like, right, I know
I think it's like, yeah, like.'

'So you guys, like, Right?
Like, it's your life like, right?'

'Yeah, no cool, like right, like, so, you wanna, right, like, like
You wanna like, sleep with me, like, tonight?'

'Like, yeah, right. OK, Like.'

'Yeah. Like, alright, like'

'Like, right, like it feels right?'

'Like, right, yeah, ok, right, like.'

'Right. Ok, like, Tonight. Right?'

THE YANK ON THE BOAT

All the way there
to Gili Air
the Yank on the boat
prattled on,
about how great drugs were
and her latest affair
I wanted to cut her throat.

HOW ARE YOU TODAY?

Hey Mumma, you want coke?
I get you mushroom? ICE?
You want I get you smoke?
Very good. No rubbish.
Crystal meth?

Hello lady, you want drink?
Strong mushroom shake?
You say yes, ok?
No worries, good stuff, yes?
You like hash cake?

Sexy lady. Hey!
I got you very good
Ticket to the moon today.
You like sit?
You want nice watch,
I get you DVD,
What is your name?

Hello Ma'am.
How are you today?
Where you stay?
Nice bag for party?
I bring it, you want, ok?

Hello Madam. Coke?
Nice Weed. Smoke?
Mumma, you want something?
Anything. You can trust me.

'I wonder, then,
I'd really love,
Not a pot but just a cup,
 A simple cup of tea.'

ISLAND LIFE

Wooden tables, painted white;
Checked cloth napkins, folded tight;
Crackle-glazing, candle bright;
Pine slat decking, fading light;
Lapping ocean, beneath feet;
Cooked to order, chargrilled meat.

Bulging vests; tattooed yobs;
Shaven heads, chomping gobs;
Wet-glass beers, silent chat;
Too much chilli, 'fuck that'.
Slouching back, ketchup splat;
iPhone pick-up, Tinder twat.

BREAKFAST IN PARADISE

A silent woman slides a plate
In front of a muscle bound gob.
'I said eggs, not rice,' carbs irritate
A steroid-full self-obsessed yob.

His bitch, who cowers in his shade
Says she was spiked and drugged.
'You say the fucker pulled a blade?'
'I could have been raped and mugged.
I'm telling you, don't fuck with me,
I've researched like fuck, online;
There's no police, the fuckers are free,
They'll fuck-off your life for a line.'
'Can I get my order now?
I've waited a whole fucking hour.'

Listening in I wonder how
much more of the earth they'll devour.

ACT FIVE

TOMORROW'S I

As the sun began its slow descent,
colours split by shallow cloud,
kissing redoubling waves,
taking her breath,
holding her gaze,
the man two empty tables
distant to her right,
peppering his eggs and ham,
salting deep fried chips,
broke into her reverie:
'It's not so good tonight;
the cloud's not shelved
but other times,
when thicker layers of cumulus
disperse the evening sun,
the colours are miraculous'.
Tomorrow's I might simply smile,
protective of the moment's peace
but then a wave of empathy
washed over the silent night,
today's I, Florence Nightingale,
sorry for the shambling soul,
two tables to her right:
'You come here often, obviously'
her quip ironic reference
to clichés, chat up lines,
amateur clumsy repartee
which the hopeful, hapless use,
designed to disabuse the man
of fantasies that he might have
of walks beneath the fiery sky
with this evening's I.
'I have a house just up the road,
you're holidaying here alone?'
This evening's I had fuelled his quest
to find a confidante.
'You don't mind if I join you?
You'll find those prawns impossible
to eat in a feminine way.
We'll be a great pair,

85

you and me,
your fishy hands
and me with this garlic bread.
I asked them for some butter
but they brought me this instead'.
He told her that his name was Jeff;
his wife neither cooked nor washed or cleaned,
or let him share her bed.
Eleven years, a loveless state,
fragile finance binding them
they lived as if best friends
but if he sought to separate
she'd surely leave him destitute;
he didn't dare risk poverty
at the hands of his third cold wife.
He garbled endless tragedies,
saying he wished he'd known
she'd been enjoying solitude,
thirteen evenings' dinners
they'd have shared
had he found her sooner,
never having met someone
with eyes the deepest jade,
or blue,
he couldn't tell in candlelight,
although it was quite plain to him,
today's kind I was sent to ease
his loneliness and pain.
He didn't ask her name
but as she slipped away,
he warned tomorrow's I
that he'd be there again;
he hoped she'd meet him
for a drink
and watch the sun sink gracefully,
kissing the eyes which gazed,
an azure blue,
he could see them now,
mirroring dancing waves.

RELATIVITY

'Don't cry!
You'll be back soon', they say,
'You'll dive amongst the Manta Ray,
Together watch the sinking sun,
The world's so small today'.
But now, aboard a tiny craft,
The earth seems alien and vast,
The distance from my sunny son
Extended by my overdraft.

LONG HAUL IN THE CHEAP SEATS

The journey makes its way into its final hour
regathering boundaries to us:
That arm that strayed in its sleep into the space of the next seat, pulled
back; the watch twisted on the wrist, the hand run through the hair.
The night that chased out, traced, Dark's shroud across the planet, evoked
Doom's prophesies.
The sun cold, packed in baggage hold,
that all modesties held dear, those bashful preserves of first love, taboos
were broken, here:
that mouth gaping; sulphurous waking, twisted aching.
Debris discarded –
the tissues, the wet wipes,
tiny tins, the straws;
flight socks, headphones,
tables safely stored;
Currency resorted; paper-coins souvenired.
Babies, re-nappied. Toddlers' sore ears.
Barbie in the middle aisle is finally seeing red.
She'd have liked a little notice before they'd woken her with breakfast,
They had made her feel like cargo; she knew the service she'd expected.
'Don't just suddenly turn the lights on and serve the bloody food! They're
supposed to give us notice' scanning, nodding 'you'll collude' saying,
'bloody rude'.
Another, to my right, with whom I shared the night,
a humid unknown shoulder facing into cheek,
until, intruding, turbulence's vacuum,
unsucked skin,
now, passing coffee, sugar, Panadol to the far left seat,
risks momentary exchange - eyes meet –
as we anticipate our journey's end begin.
We didn't speak, would not have dared,
before the intimacy shared, in case, in such a static situation, well just
suppose, 'we might have been':
but taxi-ed over tarmac eyebrows signal we agree,
passing bags over heads, seat backs, bruising bartered duty-free,
our singular, high-principled similarity: that she, I acknowledge, we are
grateful, we had turned out not to be - Barbie.
Grounded. Cell division. Parted.
Regathering boundaries to us.

DEAR LORD AND FATHER OF MANKIND

(For Joan Allen, 1923-2018, a warm well of love.)

Mon leant over half way through
As I sobbed my singing of
'Interpreted by love',
'Me next, I spect,
But I don't mind,
I've lived a lovely life'.
And Pat, trapped,
Her body now a cage,
'Nothing wrong except my Age;
95 and still alive,
We Bletchley girls, so many had
Fewer hours, shorter lives,
Than Mon and I, still here'.
Till not. It stops when time
Decides. 'Abide' chant
greying choirs.
Resurrected, once retired,
The vicar who, when young,
Aspired to set the living free
Through loving god,
Finds them joined in song
Singing still, 'with me'.

CURTAIN CALL

Marjorie lived to 95.
A miracle that no one died, before,
That all survived her will to drive,
Even home to her own death's door.
We laughed from pews, relief from grief,
'You must have a look in the garage
once we've laid our final wreaths'.
The living car displayed its scars,
Front, back and blindsided.
It made us laugh,
again,
returned from Crem. to sandwiches
united, knowing no-one's really sure,
how to park a car, or grieve,
or when they'll know
it's time to leave
the driving to another.

EPILOGUE

WHEN YOU GO

When you go, tomorrow,
I will never have known greater sorrow.
Now, its kiss, yours, is joy's epitaph;
each breath, each step, tomorrow's photograph.

BIOGRAPHY

DEFERRED

Have you spent your life deferring,
Conditioning's Mistress?
Floating off to find yourself,
thinking that you're on the shelf,
drifting back to dredge up that
which you'd left for later?
Meaning to, knowing that, you'd do it,
once you'd done that thing for him,
should the kids' feet, hearts, heads, lice,
life-foul injuries allow,
but after watching 'News at One'
and tweeting so the world would know
you knew which way was up, although,
once your mother'd had her 'op,
you wouldn't have her weekly shop
or to hide your grief,
once she'd told you that she knew,
has been hiding hers from you,
once she'd saved you both from drowning;
once the boat's re-readied and un-holed,
stern turned, broadside to tragedy;
once the light has switched to vapour
today's mirage you know's unreal;
once pensions and securities
are shored, remains assured
a port-out, starboard-home insured redundancy;
once the kids trawl home,
un-pack back-packs
back to start what they had stopped,
leave again, come back to say they've left;
 once you feel much less bereft;
once you've nothing left
but what you've left;
then my I, who I've deferred,
is now unearthed in words.